GILES GILBERT S
HIS SON'S VIE w

Printed in Great Britain by Zenith Media, Pontypool.

*On the Shoulders of Giants: Giles Gilbert Scott
with Richard (aged about 4), and family members*

※◆※

GILES GILBERT SCOTT
HIS SON'S VIEW

An illustrated talk given to the Art Workers Guild
on 14 December 1962

by
RICHARD GILBERT SCOTT

edited by
Penny Granger and John Martin

Liverpool Cathedral Publications

First published September 2011
Reprinted October 2011
New edition February 2015
Second Edition February 2018

Text © Richard Gilbert Scott
Editorial material © Penny Granger
Digital images © John Martin
Image retouching: Taylor Simons Design

Published by Liverpool Cathedral

Designed by Taylor Simons Design
Set in 11/14pt Sabon

ISBN 9780954395322

Contents

Sketch of Oban Cathedral by Giles Gilbert Scott

Preface

The original talk was given to the Art Workers Guild in London on 14 December 1962, nearly three years after Sir Giles Gilbert Scott's death in February 1960. The occasion was a ladies' night – one of four each year – as women were not allowed to become members of the Guild until 1967. As well as showing 80 or so slides, some of Scott's drawings were displayed around the room.

Richard Gilbert Scott's text has been lightly edited, and footnotes added to give extra detail and to update the story of Sir Giles Gilbert Scott's buildings. Dating buildings is a rather imprecise art, as it can take a decade or more from commission to opening, and the date of each stage of a project may be cited. Although other sources often vary, the dates given in this text are the author's, and the sequence of work is in chronological order.

A few of the slides are missing; the remaining 75 have been digitally scanned. These are reproduced in a separate section at the end, with corresponding numbers in the text. It is envisaged that the original slides will join Scott's papers, already held at the RIBA in London.

Sir Giles Gilbert Scott was undoubtedly one of the most important architects of the 20th century. There is as yet no published monograph on his life and work, though much information is available in architectural journals, Pevsner's *Buildings of England,* and online, not only to fill the gaps in the picture sequence that accompanied this talk, but also to give information about his many other buildings that had to be left out of the hour-long talk. It may seem surprising that there is no mention of Scott's red telephone boxes, but in the early 1960s they were not under threat, and had not yet achieved iconic status.

Website URLs cited in the footnotes were correct and active in June 2011.

The editors have been delighted to work with Richard Gilbert Scott in bringing his talk and the pictures to a wider audience.

Penny Granger
John Martin

13 July 2011
(The 200ᵗʰ anniversary of the birth of Sir George Gilbert Scott, Sir Giles Gilbert Scott's Grandfather)

Sir Giles Gilbert Scott: The Talk

Giles Gilbert Scott was born in 1880 at 26 Church Row, Hampstead, a house that Moira Shearer subsequently lived in.[1] It was his hope that he would live to see the day when a plaque would be fixed to its walls commemorating the fact that Sir Giles Scott and Moira Shearer lived there.

He was a shy, modest man with a singularly beautiful character. He instilled great affection in the hearts of those who knew him. He could be very determined, and he was an artist. An architect with a prodigious output, he is seen here *(fig 1)* working, a few months before he died. He was the grandson of Sir George Gilbert Scott and son of Gilbert Scott, the former more famous than the latter.[2] He had two brothers and a sister of whom his brother Adrian was also an architect.

He went to school at Beaumont College, chosen because his father, after examining various schools, fell in love with

[1]   Moira Shearer (1926-2006) was a strikingly attractive ballet dancer and actress.

[2]   It may justifiably be said that no county in England has been untouched by a Scott hand. For more on the older members of the dynasty, see David Cole, *The Work of Sir Gilbert Scott* (London: Architectural Press, 1980), George Gilbert Scott, *Personal and Professional Recollections: A Facsimile of the Original Edition with New Material and a Critical Introduction by Gavin Stamp* (Stamford: Paul Watkins, 1995), and Gavin Stamp, *An Architect of Promise: George Gilbert Scott Junior (1839-1897) and the Late Gothic Revival* (Donington: Shaun Tyas, 2002).

1

St John's College, which was the junior school.[3] This building, designed by John Francis Bentley, architect of Westminster Cathedral, had just been completed. It is highly ornate and so aroused the enthusiasm of my grandfather that he pronounced his boys would go there regardless of what they taught. So to Beaumont they went, and though they did some work at the College I think it would be fair to say that most of it was done after they left school! Father did receive one prize there – a book – inscribed "for natural philosophy". This was not a subject that was taught nor did he know what it meant.

My grandfather died while his sons were still at Beaumont, oddly enough in the Midland Grand Hotel at St Pancras, which had been designed by his father.[4]

The oldest boy, Sebastian, subsequently took up medicine and became an eminent radiologist. The two younger sons, Giles and Adrian, debated what they should do. Neither at that time had any particular yearning to be architects though their mother was very keen that they should be. After some discussion they decided that working in an architect's office was likely to be less exacting than any other, so they opted for architecture. On leaving school my father was articled

3   Beaumont College, Old Windsor, was a Jesuit school. It closed in 1967; St John's continues as a preparatory school.

4   The hotel closed in 1935. Saved twice from demolition, the building has been converted into apartments and a new hotel which was opened on 5 May 2011, exactly 138 years after the opening of the original hotel.

for three years to the office of Temple Moore, paying the sum of £50 per annum for the privilege.

The family at this time was living in a flat at Battersea which was large, spacious, and cheap. The payment of school fees being a problem, Father travelled to the office every day in Staple Inn, High Holborn, by a horse bus known as the Green Favourite.

Holidays and weekends were spent in Sussex at Ninfield *(fig 2)* in a house that belonged to the family on my grandmother's side. It was from here, before the advent of the motor car, that architectural excursions were made on bicycles all over the eastern part of the county, rich in churches of the 14th century. Accompanied by my Grandmother, Adrian and Father covered the countryside "steeplechasing". Staying at wayside inns they sketched, measured up and drew out anything which took their fancy.

Battle was the nearest little town: its High Street *(fig 3)* has some small scale domestic stuff and plenty of atmosphere; the gatehouse of Battle Abbey *(fig 4)*, 14th century Gothic, built in Sussex ironstone, was the very thing for their sketchbooks.

Nearby is Brede Place – an Elizabethan manor house. In places such as this where the grounds were marked 'strictly private' they obeyed their father's injunction: "Go through the gate fast and get as far as you can until you are stopped, then retire slowly looking well about."

The Jacobean doorway is where I got stopped but I retired slowly.

Etchingham Church *(fig 5)* was measured and drawn out complete. It is one of four in Sussex with a centrally placed tower, perhaps the germ of Liverpool Cathedral. There are majestic stone arches within. Other churches included Ashburnham *(fig 6)*, Westham *(fig 7)*, Westfield *(fig 8)*, Alfriston *(fig 9)* – a central tower with spire – and Penshurst *(fig 10)*. All the churches are notable for their towers; they are not high but solid and robust, with strong buttresses.

These were formative years, there was no father to guide (perhaps this was a good thing?) and I think the material gathered during these excursions provides a key to much of his work. Father always described himself as of yeoman stock and I think he was really describing the architectural values that he absorbed at this time. Strong, sturdy, unsophisticated, calm, honest, straightforward, no nonsense sort of stuff, these are the qualities of a yeoman, these are the qualities of these churches, these are the qualities that my father strove to reincarnate in his own work and generally succeeded in doing so, for he was a romantic. These buildings were the beginning of his architectural vocabulary – he was impressed!

The family at this time was still living at Battersea and it was from here in 1901 that my father entered the competition for the Anglican Cathedral at Liverpool. Up to then his creative genius had produced nothing more than a design for a pipe rack which his sister made.

Not unnaturally (for it was a prodigious task for such a young and inexperienced architect) his enthusiasm waned when his competition drawings were little more than half complete and they lay untouched, the sending-in time approaching fast. By chance a friend came to dinner and asked how it was going. Father said it wasn't and it didn't seem likely to. The drawings were produced, the friend was encouraging and the enthusiasm returned. As time had almost run out, his mother and brother Adrian were marshalled to assist him in the drawing out. Who was the friend who came to dinner? Nobody can remember except that he was a doctor – such is life![5]

The winning competition drawings *(fig 11)* show little to recognise of the Cathedral as it stands today. It had twin towers and a long nave. The design *(fig 12)* shows the west end seems to have been much influenced by the work of his father and grandfather. The Cathedral Committee was astonished to find, when the nom-de-plume envelopes were opened in 1902, that it had awarded first place to an architect aged 22 who was a Roman Catholic. It therefore, not unwisely I think, asked George Frederick Bodley, one of the Assessors, to act

---

5   The friend was Giles's cousin, Henry Cooper. See Peter Kenneley, *The Building of Liverpool Cathedral*, 4th edn (Lancaster: Carnegie, 2008), p14. For more on Liverpool Cathedral, see also Vere Cotton, *The Book of Liverpool Cathedral* (Liverpool: Liverpool University Press, 1964).

6   Bodley had been articled to Giles's grandfather, Sir George Gilbert Scott, who was a relative by marriage.

with him.[6] This proved a very uneasy partnership *(fig 13)*, one which my father sought to bring to an end by offering his resignation. The letter of resignation was never placed before the Committee owing to the fact of Bodley's death just before its meeting. The lower part of the Lady Chapel at Liverpool is the result of this duet.

After the success of Liverpool, there being no further school bills to pay, the family betook itself off to Tavistock Square where, to quote my uncle, "they lived in style with a butler and his wife and three maids." The Scotts, it seemed, had arrived. They dressed for dinner every night and only drank wine.

If Father hoped that winning Liverpool would result in a rush of commissions he was doomed to disappointment. The first building he acted as architect for was the Clerk of Works' hut on the site at Liverpool and he wasn't proud of it. He did not receive his next commission until 1910 which was for a small church in Sheringham, Norfolk. The intervening years were spent working on the drawings of Liverpool and a certain amount of travelling in Spain and France. These were the days of Norman Shaw who was the doyen of the profession at that time.[7] Father produced a series of little pen and ink drawings of imaginary edifices, all in the classical style; these came to be known as "dad's drunks" (figs 14, 15, 16). They were splurges of the imagination, very

---

7   See Andrew Saint, *Richard Norman Shaw*, rev. edn (New Haven and London: Yale University Press, 2010).

6

romantic and probably inspired by Piranesi's prison plates.[8]

In Spain he was much influenced by what he saw there. He learned the value of concentrated ornament as a contrast to plain walling and this theme dominated his work throughout his life. The main reredos in Liverpool is directly attributable to that in the Church of St Nicholas in Burgos.

In 1911 the church at Sheringham was built; it looks rather bleak *(fig 17)* in its newness. It is one of his very few churches that has no tower. It is a little church with an element of bigness in it; also illustrated *(fig 18)* are the altar and reredos.

In 1912 came a church in Bournemouth[9] and a convent in Harrow.

In 1913 came one of his rare houses: at 129 Grosvenor Road for Sir Oliver Stanley. 129 Grosvenor Road is on the Embankment, nearly opposite Dolphin Court, directly on the riverside. It is now a nightclub.[10] The client and architect paid

---

8   The Italian artist Giovanni Battista Piranesi (1720–78) was famous for his etchings of Rome and of fictitious and atmospheric *Carceri d'Invenzione*.

9   The Roman Catholic Church of the Annunciation. For more on this, see www.users.globalnet.co.uk/~pencot/history.htm including the text of a letter from Scott about the project.

10   129 Grosvenor Road has since been demolished and replaced by a block of luxury apartments.

a visit to Italy together for the purpose of gathering ideas. Looking at the outside, however *(fig 19)*, it does not seem that the visit was very fruitful. The interior *(figs 20, 21)* is a different matter. One can guess where they went: Naples and Pompeii. The client was disabled and the house, planned around an internal court in the Roman manner, is, apart from the servants' bedrooms, all on one floor. The flower bed in the middle was originally a swimming pool but never used, so it was filled in. It was the habit of the bargees at high tide to put their hands over the wall and take the cushions lying on the garden furniture by the river front.

In 1914 the Church of Our Lady in Northfleet was built: in brick with a magnificent tower *(figs 22, 23)*. No doubt the successful solution that he achieved here gave him the confidence to tackle the greatest of all his towers at Liverpool.

Also in 1914 came St Paul's, Derby Lane, Liverpool *(fig 24)*. This seems to have a kind of Belgian touch about it with its curious roof pitches. It was at this time that he spent his holidays in Knokke in Belgium where there was a fine golf course.

Between 1919 and 1935 he designed hosts of war memorials, including a fine one at Wigan *(fig 25)*.

In 1921 came his first work at Ampleforth – the church there. Ampleforth Abbey church was built in two stages, the second stage being completed only in 1961 after his death. Because of the great increase in building costs between 1922 and 1958 it was impossible to complete the church in the rather elaborate style of the first part. The illustration *(fig 26)* is a drawing of the church as completed. The plan is that of a cross; the three remaining arms and tower were completed later. The arms were not carried through to their full height along their length as was the original intention. Internally the first part is elaborate and beautifully detailed. The photograph of the reredos (fig 27), seen through an archway, gives an indication of the richness of the detail employed. The style is Father's Romanesque and the stone is Blue Hornton. The second stage had none of this elaboration, being carried out with the minimum of stone dressings and simplified plastered piers.

1922 saw St Maughold's, Ramsay, Isle of Man *(fig 28)*, with its magnificent tower and unusual presbytery adjoining – perhaps there is a little bit of Lutyens in it with its tall chimneys. These chimneys worried the architect, for whenever he saw a photograph of the group he would instinctively blot them out with his finger.

In 1923 there were additions to the nave at Downside Abbey, and the completion of the tower. It was in that year that a more domestic side to his practice commenced, beginning with Clare College, Cambridge, in the classical style.[11] This building *(fig 29)* has a small domestic scale and intimate charm that is wholly endearing. It is a very attractive building, very successful.

---

11   Clare Memorial Court, Queen's Road; Scott later designed an extension to the original building, in the same style.

9

Also in 1923 came further commissions with the first of several school houses at Ampleforth. In 1925 Charterhouse chapel – of Bargate stone – a 'fortress church' *(fig 30)* was built by direct labour under the school Clerk of Works. All except Sir Giles believed that this building would not have sufficient daylight. He had great difficulty convincing the Building Committee that this would not be the case but finally got his way. It exemplified his interest in natural lighting, and he was always experimenting. He said he could never make his churches dark however hard he tried. The photograph of the interior *(fig 31)* gives no indication of the magnificent proportions and grand atmosphere.

In the same year came his own house in London *(fig 32)*, rather in the Clare manner.[12] From his early sketches for this house he was obviously much torn between the Roman style developed for Sir Oliver Stanley's house in Grosvenor Road and that of Clare College. Father had waited patiently for 12 years to obtain the lease of this property which was then stables.

In 1927 came an infirmary for the school at Ampleforth, and a house there for a Mrs Romanes. Mrs Romanes was by report a most frightening woman, and Father studiously avoided meeting her. When the house had reached first floor level the client declared she had not approved the plan and insisted on the staircase being reversed. This was because apple storage was required in the roof! When the house was complete Father paid a surreptitious visit at a time when he

---

[12]   Chester House, Clarendon Place, London W2 2NP.

knew the client was away. The house was locked but with the aid of a penknife he got in by the dining room window. After his inspection he made notes and left by the way he had entered – through the window. At the office he was unable to find his notes and it was not until a few days later when he received an angry letter from the client, describing him amongst other things as a second class burglar, that he realised that he had left his notes on the dining room table.

Also in 1927 came two more churches – All Saints, New Brighton and St Michael's, Ashford, Middlesex. This latter church *(fig 33)* was one of my father's favourites. It was built in two stages, the second stage being completed in 1960. It is in Italian style with a pantile roof. The tower is asymmetrically placed, two thirds along the length of the nave. The interior *(fig 34)* is interesting for the inward slope given to the upper part of the nave walls, and the raising of the sanctuary floor level some 4ft above the nave floor.

My father exercised great mastery of detail. It should be remembered that all the work he did throughout his life was entirely drawn out by him to full size.

The reredos at St Anne's, Accrington[13] illustrates his liking of rich things against plain backgrounds. Here is mastery of detail: scholarship combined with creative genius; the wall is filled richly and yet so effortlessly. Pictured *(fig 35)* is a small reredos he designed for the same church. Also in this period he designed Cardinal Gasquet's tomb at Downside; it was

---

13   He was not responsible for the church.

another of his favourites *(figs 36, 37)*. And in 1928 he built an extension in stone for Magdalen College, Oxford.[14] His feeling for wood and stone probably developed from his early contact with 14th century Gothic in Sussex. That was a period notable for its fine craftsmanship, perhaps the peak of Gothic detail, where decoration was suited to its purpose and strictly related to its structure.

In 1928 came the Salvation Army headquarters at Denmark Hill *(fig 38)*.[15] One is certainly impressed by the fine massing of the administration building in the centre. Flanked by two plain blocks, it piles up with grandeur with its great area of plain walling. In the centre the great tower 35ft square rises up to over 200 feet. The whole scheme covers an area of 7 acres and it is composed of blocks of buildings, each acting independently of one another. There is perhaps a certain monotony about the treatment of the individual buildings. As they are really separate, one might have supposed greater variation would have been permissible without destroying the unity of the whole.

The tower has an affinity with that of St Francis, Terriers, a flint church in High Wycombe *(fig 39)*. The interior view

14   Longwall Quad, continuing Bodley's 1879-84 buildings which form St Swithun's Quad.

15   William Booth Memorial Training College. Scott was consultant architect, responsible for the design of the exterior and assembly hall; he also supervised the selection of external building materials.

shows that the lighting of this church is achieved entirely by windows in the side aisle *(fig 40)*. The Presbytery *(fig 41)* is a fall from grace, I think.

In 1930 came another flint church at Broadstairs *(fig 42)*, a very unusual arrangement of tower and tall apse-like sanctuary. The donor, a very old lady, sat all day, every day, in a little wooden shelter on the site watching the church being built. Also that year was built the chapel of Lady Margaret Hall at Oxford. The college has brick buildings, rather similar in style to those that Father designed for Whitelands College, Putney. Whitelands is a very large building which has been given a domestic character – the chapel interior is full of rather interesting detail.[16]

This was a busy year for all, and there was another church, of St Alphege at Bath. The exterior of the church is stone built in an Italian style. The interior *(fig 43)* is very fine – the lighting is quite opposite to that of St Francis, Terriers, being at the clerestory level only. The picture also shows details of some of the capitals in the nave. Gough was the name of the carver.[17]

---

16   Whitelands College is now part of Roehampton University. Its Putney site was vacated in 2005, buildings designed by the author in the 1960s demolished, and the original building converted into luxury apartments. In the chapel, Scott had incorporated stained glass and a reredos by William Morris from the earlier college chapel in Chelsea; this had been resited in the college's new home, Parkstead House. See www.roehampton.ac.uk/whitelands/history

17   William D. Gough, who also did work for Ninian Comper, made carvings and statuary for Scott at Brighton, Ampleforth, and Liverpool before those at St Alphege, Bath. One of his capitals

Next is a perspective of a design for a parish church in Stoke on Trent, cathedral-like in its size *(fig 44)*. It was never carried out and I don't know the history of it but I believe there were problems of finance.

Building began on Cambridge University Library in 1931. I think the close proximity of Clare Memorial Court led to a rather self-conscious effort to disassociate one building from the other with a not too successful result *(fig 45)*.[18]

In 1931 came the church of St Alban's, Golders Green *(figs 46, 47)*. In 1932 came St Andrew's Church, Luton – a striking brick-built church *(figs 48, 49, 50)* with great strong buttresses supporting cross arches – clerestory lighting again *(fig 51)*. Here *(fig 52)* is a detail of the doors showing the adze marks – very Sussex, this.

In the same year came Oban Cathedral *(fig 53)*. It is really a large granite-built parish church.

In 1934 came extensions to Trinity Hall, Cambridge,[19] and in

---

···   bears likenesses of architect, carver, and other persons associated with the building of the church. See www.saintalphege.org.uk

18   After visiting the University Library in 2010 the author declared that he had revised his opinion upwards! He recalls being taken as a small boy with his father to see the foundations of the library – which, as the architect was dismayed to discover, were built a few feet off centre. But the view through Clare Memorial Court is now obscured by a new college library.

19   A building in North Court.

1935 the first of his industrial works – Battersea Power Station *(fig 54)*. The fourth chimney is now complete and if there is criticism to be made of the four chimneys being placed at each corner of the building in a seemingly rather forced manner I would say that this was the result of an engineering requirement and not a request of the architect. Father was not called in until after the foundations had been laid.[20]

Also in 1935 came the Guinness Brewery at Park Royal *(fig 55)* – probably the best of his industrial ventures,[21] and then came Waterloo Bridge *(fig 56)* as compared with the original design *(fig 57)*.

A year later saw the controversial New Bodleian Library at Oxford. I quote from a letter published in the *Oxford Times* at the time:

"Dear Sir, By courtesy of the Bodleian officials I was allowed to see the plans for the new Bodleian and I think no stone should be left unturned to prevent such a building ever being erected.

"Each new building in Oxford seems uglier than the last and the plans for the new Bodleian are in my opinion simply hideous." The letter finished up with: "it should not be difficult to combine beauty with utility. The art of

---

20   Scott was consultant architect for the exterior. In 2014 work began on developing the long-derelict site into an "urban village".

21   Closed in 2005 and demolished in 2006.

architecture demands beauty but the new library if ever erected (which God forbid) will I consider be a perpetual eyesore to the city and an insult to the old Bodleian. Yours truly, S.S. Cotton, Vicar of Wootton."

The doorway shows the Spanish influence *(fig 58)*. It is a very large building, holding some 5 million volumes, and is larger than the library at Cambridge.[22] I think the architect has very successfully disguised its size, for it is a colossal building, and he has managed to keep the scale and massing down to very reasonable proportion and, in doing so, paying respect to its surroundings in the heart of the city.

In 1937 he designed a chapel at Bromsgrove School which was finally completed in 1960. It is reminiscent of a rather large Sussex barn. He was also doing some work at Downside and Ampleforth. In 1938 he was working on a design for the Town Hall at Dolgelly in Wales *(fig 59)*. This is a charming design in stone which never saw the light of day. The war intervened and the plans were shelved.

In 1939 an office building for the electricity authority in Bristol was started, and completed after the war *(fig 60)*. It seems to me to typify my father's unhappiness in dealing with this type of work. There was too much window area required, not enough opportunity for great areas of blank

---

[22] The brief for Cambridge was also for 5 million volumes; its site just outside the city centre is much larger and not cramped as at Oxford. The New Bodleian – renamed the Weston Library – with many original features restored, now houses Special Collections, while the main body of books is stored in a warehouse in Swindon.

wall and too little excuse for punching in concentrated ornament. The office block did not fit the well established theme. Copthorne Court, a block of flats in Maida Vale, is also a case in point.[23]

Power stations were a different matter: they lent themselves to vast areas of brick wall which were so beloved by him, and he was able to concentrate his ornament in horizontal lines. Pictured *(fig 61)* is a detail at Bankside Power Station, built in the 1950s but it is typical of this type of ornamentation.[24]

The success of this style prompted him to try it out on the Guildhall office blocks for the City of London Corporation *(fig 62)*, but again there were too many windows, and the effect he strove for does not come through. In spite of this, however, his eye for massing and proportion remains as sure as ever.

During the war he sat on the Royal Academy Replanning Committee and subsequently became its chairman, succeeding Edwin Lutyens. He was absorbed by traffic

---

23   There, as always, paying attention to the provision of natural light, Scott designed a jutting out frontage to the building which reduced the need for light wells.

24   Bankside is now triumphantly reincarnated as Tate Modern. See Rowan Moore and Raymund Ryan, with contributions by Adrian Hardwicke and Gavin Stamp, *Building Tate Modern: Herzog & De Meuron transforming Giles Gilbert Scott* (London: Tate Gallery, 2000).

problems and the plan which his Committee produced *(fig 63)* proposed a ring road connecting the main railway stations north and south of the river, running through Hyde Park to the West and by the Tower of London to the East. The ring road was a low level motorway connected to a secondary traffic system by means of ramps, overpasses and underpasses. There was not a roundabout on it. In addition it was proposed to connect the main line railway stations by means of an underground railway system. It was envisaged that passengers passing through London and beyond would be able to do so without changing trains.[25]

After the destruction of Coventry he was commissioned to produce designs for the new cathedral there. His proposals bestrode the ruins of the old cathedral, retaining the tower and apse at the east end *(fig 64)*. The original interior was of conventional design with stone piers and arches with plaster walls and infillings rather similar to Charterhouse chapel. The design, however, was too conventional for the Bishop who wanted something more modern, and the interior was changed *(fig 65)*. This aroused considerable controversy, the change being carried out without any alteration to the design of the exterior. We see the Spanish theme again, the plain walls and the punch of decoration with the baldachino over the centrally placed altar. How this would have flowered had there been the opportunity! The Fine Arts Commission, of

25   *Road, Rail and River in London: The Royal Academy Planning Committee's Second Report, with a Foreword by Sir Giles Gilbert Scott, R.A., Chairman of the Committee* (London: Country Life, 1944). Sir Giles would doubtless have been pleased to hear of the Thameslink and Crossrail projects.

which my father had been a member, rejected this proposal and my father resigned his commission. In a letter to *The Times* he complained of the interference that he had suffered during the whole affair, bringing about conditions which made it impossible for an artist to do his work. The conditions nevertheless had stimulated his mind to produce what was for him a completely new idea – this arch form – and he was very intrigued with it.

It was used in the approach viaduct to the Forth Road Bridge *(fig 66)*, and variations on the theme were produced in a church at Preston, Lancashire in 1956, and the Carmelite church in Kensington in 1957, within a stone's throw of his grandfather's church at the bottom of Church Street. The interior view *(fig 67)* shows the concentration of ornament at the altar, the plain walls, all here together with the arch form which was first suggested at Coventry.

Shortly after the war he was engaged upon the rebuilding of the House of Commons *(fig 68)*. It is chiefly notable for the prodigious amount of detailing that went into it – all again drawn out to full size right down to inkwells, paperweights, and loudspeakers in the form of Tudor roses.

In 1947 he was engaged upon designs for Rye House Power Station *(fig 69)* and one at the Aswan Dam in Egypt. This was before the Russians got in, and subsequently the scheme was abandoned. His power stations were really all variations on the same theme. At Bankside *(fig 70)* the second half is still being built. They were mistakenly called "cathedral like" but he had no such conception in his mind that they should

19

be so. They were opportunities for the plain brick "the most difficult thing in the world to build", he said. He always strove for symmetry wherever he could: "it is in accord with the higher forms of nature" was his explanation. He marvelled at nature and took constant delight in the structure of plants and weeds, specimens of which he was for ever bringing home for examination.

One of the more successful of his post-war works was the restoration of the roof of the Guildhall in London *(fig 71)*. This building has had on it no fewer than four roofs at different times. The original roof, of which there was no evidence, was destroyed during the Fire of London, after which Wren put on a roof of classical design; this was subsequently removed by the Victorians who commissioned Horace Jones to put on a hammer beam type of roof to emulate Westminster Hall. This was subsequently destroyed by fire in World War II and Father was commissioned by the Corporation of London to put on another one. I know that he tried another hammer beam roof truss. The Building Committee, led by Banister Fletcher, certainly wanted one but Father was unhappy, he couldn't get it right, then suddenly it hit him that the Hall with its stone shafts was designed originally for stone arches. The result *(fig 72)* is stone arches on stone piers looking as natural as if they had been there since the 14th century.

In 1952 he built a chapel for Trinity College, Toronto University in Canada, and had been employed on and off for a number of years for the Forth Road Bridge, now nearing completion. In 1956 and 1957 the churches in Preston and

Kensington that I have already mentioned were designed, and the last chapter finally closed with a little church in Plymouth.[26] He designed this, his last work, in hospital a few days before his death.

I have made no reference, apart from at the beginning, to Liverpool Cathedral. The story began there and in a sense it ends there. After the death of Bodley in 1907 the young architect was on his own with a growing sense of dissatisfaction with his design. With the experience that came his way and the confidence that must have come with it, he completely redesigned the building, doing away with the twin towers and substituting the great central tower in their place. Pictured is an old perspective showing the present design in embryo (fig 73). The new plan has a single tower *(fig 74)* and a vast central space. This conception was presented to the Buildings Committee in 1910 and in spite of the fact that some of the foundations for the original scheme had been laid, the committee, to the architect's professed astonishment, accepted this new scheme. And finally the completion of the whole conception – the west end *(fig 75)*.

To sum up: I think one is entitled to ask how it was that a man who lived in such a period as ours with its great technical advances contrived throughout his life to reflect so little of it in his work. The answer lies, I think, in his desire to reincarnate values which were to him eternal. Serenity, calmness and harmony: he strove to get his buildings to say

26   The Roman Catholic Church of Christ the King, now the Catholic Chaplaincy for the University of Plymouth.

these things. He didn't care much how he got them, the end justified the means, his vocabulary was basically Gothic, and modern means of construction, though necessary, never had any interest for him. As an architect of another generation I think this was a pity – for he had genius.

A portrait of Giles Gilbert Scott by Reginald Grenville Eves in 1935 from the RIBA Library Drawings and Archive Collections.

Postscript[27]

My father never spoke to me about creating architecture. It may seem strange, for my wife and I lived with him for 11 years after my mother died, and I was an aspiring architect. All he said to me was "proportion and scale are of paramount importance". And of course he had an instinctive sense of both these qualities.

---

[27]   Added by the author in 2011

Reproductions of 75 of the original slides used by the author in his talk to the Artworkers Guild on 14 December 1962.

Fig 1: Sir Giles Gilbert Scott

Fig 2: Hollis Street Farm, Ninfield, Sussex

Fig 3: High Street, Battle

Fig 4: Battle Abbey Gatehouse

Fig 5: Etchingham Church

Fig 6: Ashburnham Church

Fig 7: Westham Church

Fig 8: Westfield Church

Fig 9: Alfriston Church

Fig 10: Penshurst Church

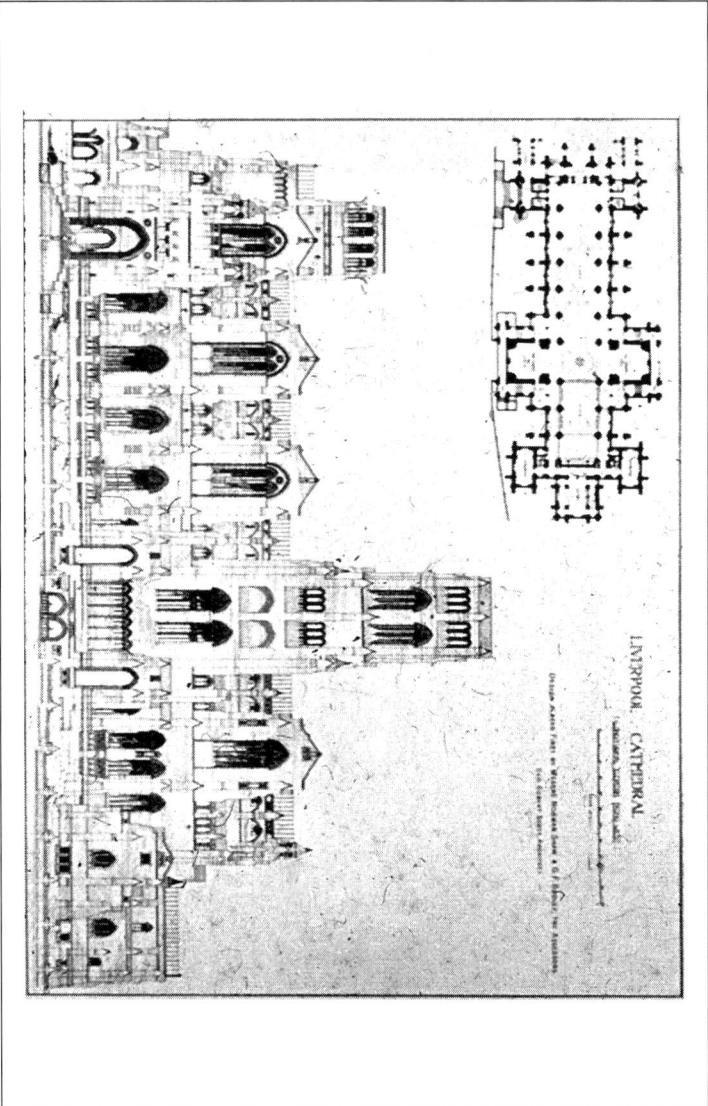

Fig 11: Liverpool Cathedral, original drawing

Fig 12: Liverpool Cathedral, unfinished west end

Fig 13: Bodley and Scott

Fig 14: "Dad's Drunks"

Fig 15: "Dad's Drunks"

Fig 16: "Dad's Drunks"

Fig 17: Sheringham Roman Catholic Church

Fig 18: Sheringham Roman Catholic Church (interior)

Fig 19: 129 Grosvenor Road, London

Fig 20: 129 Grosvenor Road, London

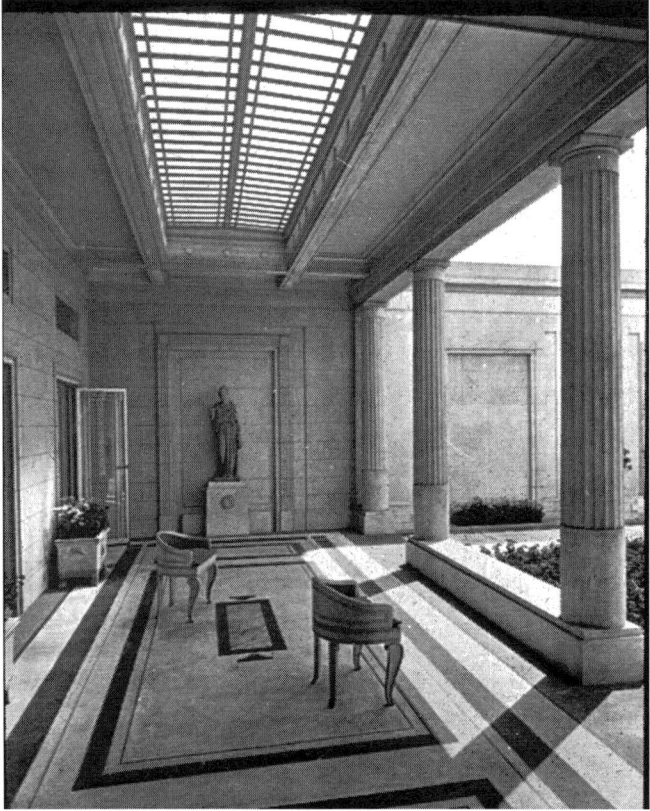

Fig 21: 129 Grosvenor Road, London

Fig 22: Roman Catholic Church of Our Lady, Northfleet

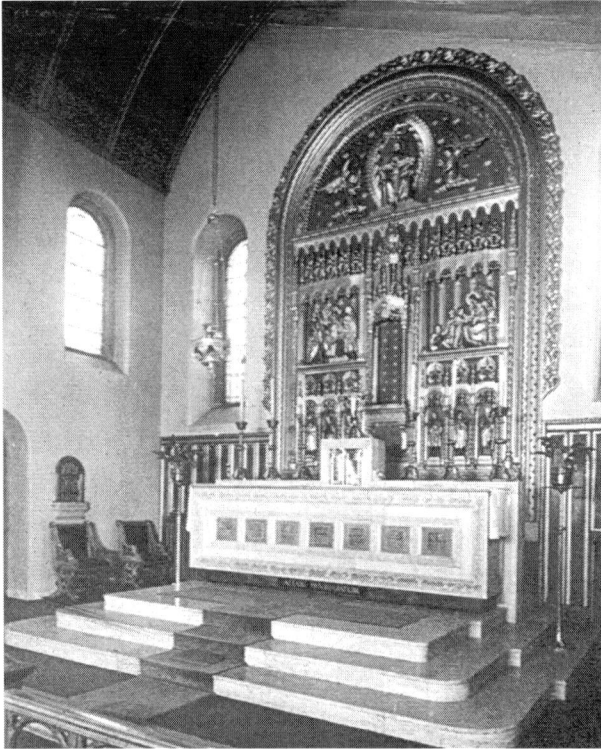

Fig 23: Roman Catholic Church of Our Lady, Northfleet (interior)

Fig 24: St Paul's, Derby Lane, Liverpool

Fig 25: Wigan War Memorial

Fig 26: Ampleforth Abbey Church

Fig 27: Ampleforth Abbey Church (interior)

Fig 28: St. Maughold's, Ramsay, Isle of Man

Fig 29: Clare Memorial Court, Cambridge

Fig 30: Charterhouse School Chapel

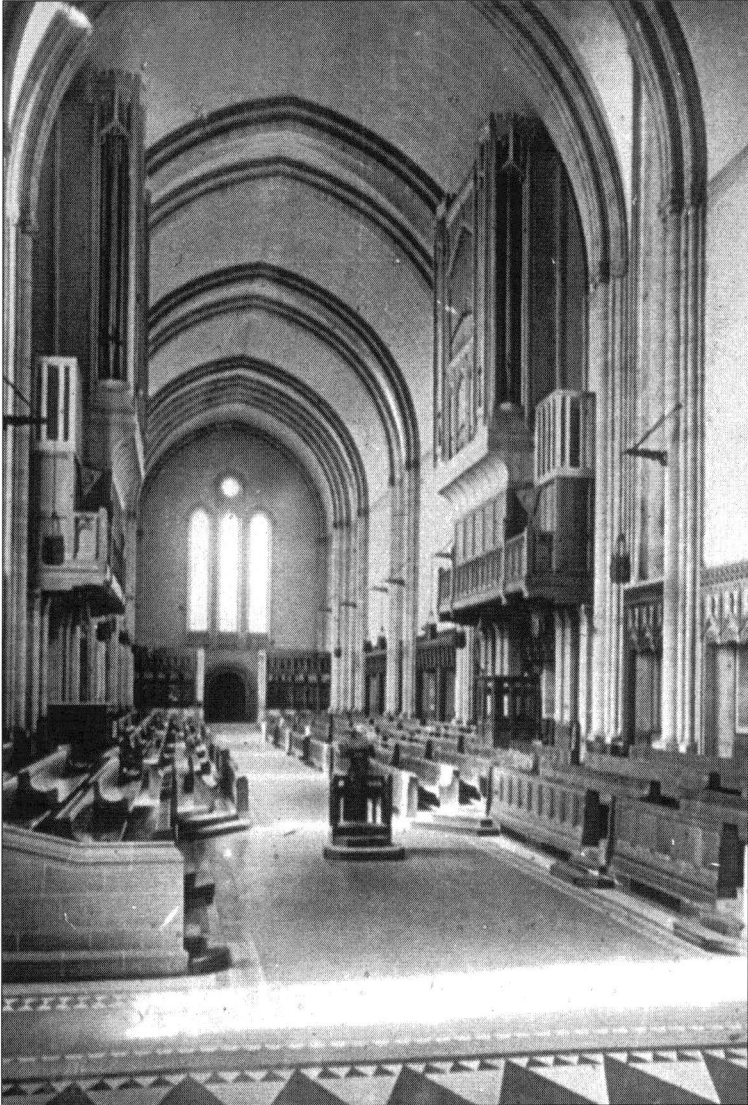

Fig 31: Charterhouse School Chapel (interior)

Fig 32: Chester House, London

Fig 33: St. Michael's, Ashford, Middlesex

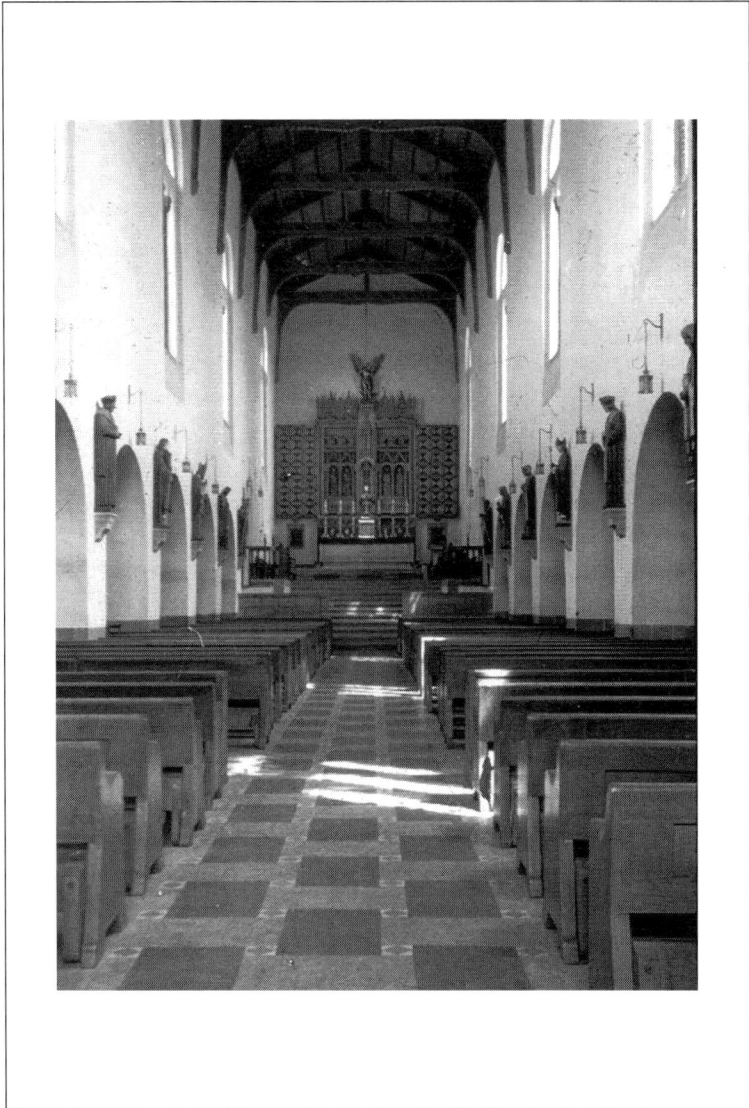

Fig 34: St. Michael's, Ashford, Middlesex (interior)

Fig 35: Reredos at St. Anne's, Accrington

Fig 36: Cardinal Gasquet's Tomb, Downside

Fig 37: Cardinal Gasquet's Tomb, Downside (detail)

55

Fig 38: William Booth Memorial College, Denmark Hill, London

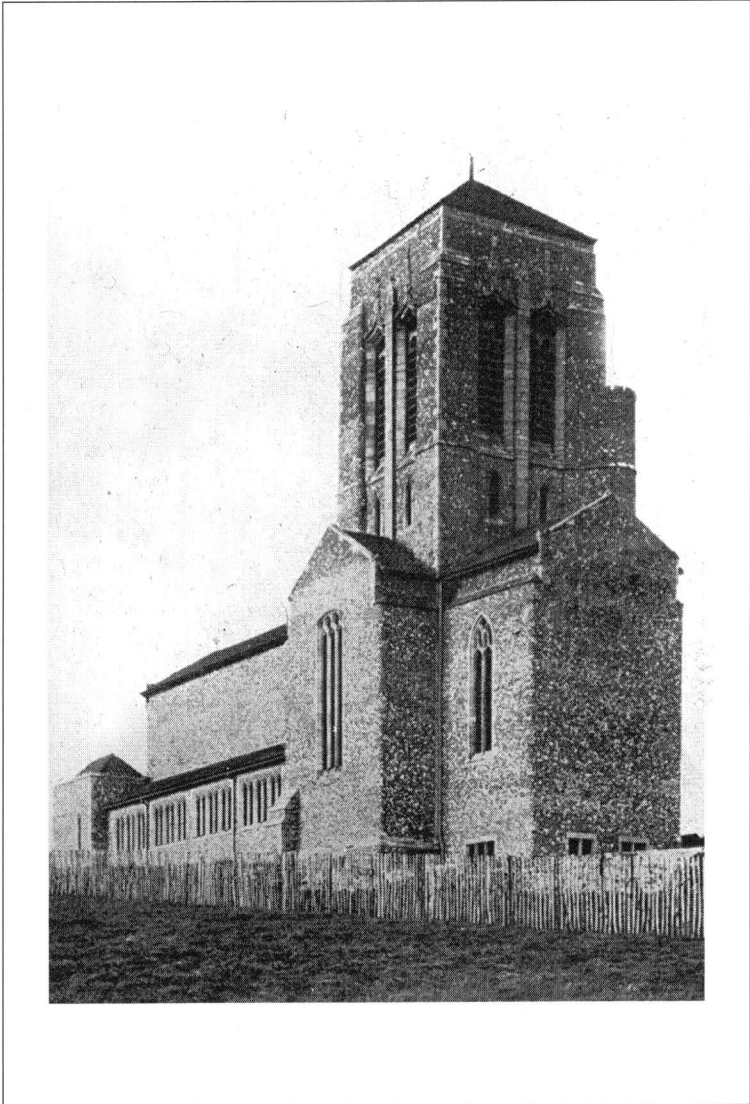

Fig 39: St. Francis's, Terriers, High Wycombe

Fig 40: St. Francis's, Terriers, High Wycombe (interior and east end)

Fig 41: St. Francis's, Terriers, High Wycombe (presbytery and church)

Fig 42: Broadstairs Roman Catholic Church

Fig 43: St. Alphege's, Bath

Fig 44: Design for a parish church, Stoke-on-Trent

Fig 45: Cambridge University Library from Clare Memorial Court

Fig 46: St. Alban's, Golders Green

Fig 47: St. Alban's, Golders Green (interior)

Fig 48: St. Andrew's, Luton

Fig 49: St. Andrew's, Luton

Fig 50: St. Andrew's, Luton (west end)

Fig 51: St. Andrew's, Luton (interior)

Fig 52: St. Andrew's, Luton (door detail)

Fig 53: Sketch of Oban Cathedral

Fig 54: Battersea Power Station, London

Fig 55: Guinness Brewery, Park Royal, London

69

Fig 56: Waterloo Bridge, London

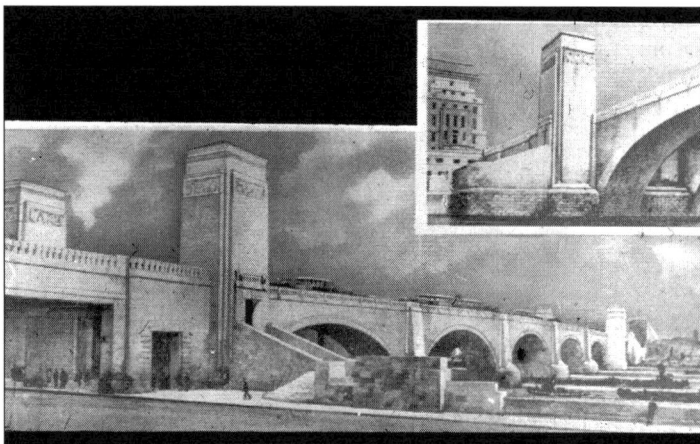

Fig 57: Original drawings for Waterloo Bridge

Fig 58: New Bodleian Library, Oxford

Fig 59: Design for Town Hall, Dolgelly, Wales

71

Fig 60: Electricity House, Bristol

Fig 61: Bankside Power Station, London (detail)

Fig 62: Guildhall office block, London

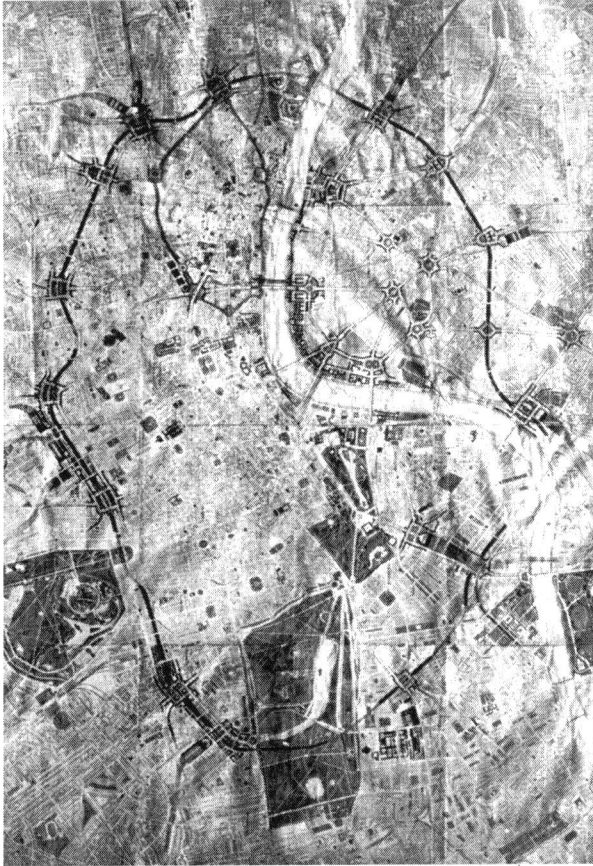

Fig 63: Plan for London (Royal Academy Replanning Committee)

Fig 64: Design for Coventry Cathedral

Fig 65: Design for Coventry Cathedral (interior)

Fig 66: Approach viaduct to the Forth Road Bridge, Scotland

Fig 67: Carmelite Church, Kensington, London (interior)

Fig 68: House of Commons, London

Fig 69: Rye House Power Station, Hoddesdon, Hertfordshire

Fig 70: Bankside Power Station, London

Fig 71: Guildhall, London

Fig 72: Guildhall, London (interior)

Fig 73: Liverpool Cathedral, new design

Fig 74: Liverpool Cathedral tower

Fig 75: Liverpool Cathedral (west end)

Index of places and buildings

Page numbers for illustrations are given in **bold**.

Index of people

Page numbers for illustrations are given in **bold.**

About the Contributors

Richard Gilbert Scott (author)

Richard Gilbert Scott, FRIBA, joined the family firm in 1949 and worked as an architect for 50 years. Among his most notable buildings are the churches of St Mark, Biggin Hill, and Our Lady, Tile Cross, Birmingham, both of which are Grade 2 listed, and the new West Wing and Art Gallery of the London Guildhall. His son Nicholas is also an architect. He and his wife Eline retired to North Norfolk, where he not only designed his own house but has also led a successful campaign to save one of his father's red K6 telephone boxes.

Penny Granger (text editor)

Penny Granger, BA, MA, PhD, is the author of a book and several articles on medieval drama; she also writes about mazes and labyrinths. While on the staff of Cambridge University Library she co-curated an exhibition on Sir Giles Gilbert Scott, marking the 75th anniversary of the opening of the library, and the 50th of Scott's death.

John Martin (technical editor)

John Martin, BSc, CEng, MIET, FHEA, is a Senior Lecturer at Anglia Ruskin University in Cambridge with interests in old photographs. He is currently engaged in the cataloguing of a collection of photographs by the Victorian photographer Martin Ridley, among whose images was one of the Church of the Annunciation in Bournemouth, designed by Sir Giles Gilbert Scott.